Praise For "Please Explain Divorce to Me!"

"In her latest book, *Please Explain Divorce to Me*, Dr. Laurie Zelinger once again delivers a high-quality, psychologically informed and child-friendly narrative. With her years of experience, Dr. Zelinger expertly navigates the sensitive topic of divorce, providing young readers with a compassionate and understanding perspective. The book's engaging storytelling, complemented by vibrant illustrations, encourages open dialogue and empowers children to navigate, with resilience and comprehension, the emotional complexities of divorce. In addition to its benefits for children, *Please Explain Divorce to Me* serves as an invaluable resource for parents, offering guidance and practical suggestions on how to approach divorce-conversations with their children, making it a comprehensive tool for the entire family."
Sarah Becker, MD, Child and Adolescent Psychiatrist,
Premium Health Center, Brooklyn, NY

"The message of Dr. Zelinger's book echoes our primary goal as divorce mediators - to assist divorcing couples to create a healthier, non-adversarial separation for the entire family. Dr. Zelinger provides parents a thoughtful, well-planned approach to gently - albeit directly - prepare their children for the news of their divorce. *Please Explain Divorce to Me* is likely to become an invaluable resource for parents to help guide them through these challenging conversations. I look forward to sharing this essential resource with the families I work with in mediation."
Maren Cardillo, Esq., Divorce Mediation Professional

"Finally… a call to arms for parents who wish to 'do it right' in navigating their children through the divorce process. Kudos to Dr. Zelinger, as she provides an excellent model for parents to follow of how to present to their children the often foreign and confusing concept of divorce. The book also provides parents with a 'cookbook,' so desperately needed, of the dos and don'ts of good parenting while going through the divorce process. Throughout the book, the underlying message to parents is to "parent up" for their children's sake."
Dr. David Lutwin, Clinical Social Worker

"The highest praise for Laurie Zelinger and her easy-to-read book, *Please Explain Divorce to Me*. As a divorce lawyer for more than 20 years, I have found that one of the most challenging issues my clients face is how to best tell their children. Laurie's book makes it easier and highlights the importance of being straight with your children, making them feel loved and secure in the face of this new configuration. It reminds parents that when they work together as a team for the best interest of their kids, they help set the stage for their children's good mental health for many years to come. When parents do not work together and speak ill of each other in front of their children, they make their children feel disloyal when they miss the other parent. Reading this book together with your children is a great first step to the rest of their lives and yours."

Judith White, Esq., specializing in divorce litigation, mediator and parent coordination

"I have had the honor and pleasure of editing for the publisher, *Loving Healing Press*, all of Dr. Laurie Zelinger's *Please Explain* illustrated children's books. Like the other books in the series, this book will delight, captivate and educate children caught in a serious situation—in this case, the divorce of their parents—while, at the same time, educating parents how to navigate through the process in a way that minimizes harm to the child. It is an added bonus that following her (research-based) advice will also minimize harm to the separating couple."

Bob Rich, Ph.D., author of 19 books, including *From Depression to Contentment: A Self-therapy Guide*.

Please Explain Divorce to Me!

Because My Parents Are Breaking Up

A Story for Children and Step-By-Step Guide for Parents

By Laurie Zelinger, PhD
Illustrated by Elisa Sabella

Loving Healing Press
Ann Arbor, MI

Please Explain Divorce to Me! Because My Parents Are Breaking Up -- A Story for Children and Step-By-Step Guide for Parents

ISBN 978-1-61599-780-0 paperback
ISBN 978-1-61599-781-7 hardcover
ISBN 978-1-61599-782-4 eBook

Library of Congress Cataloging-in-Publication Data

Names: Zelinger, Laurie, 1952- author. | Sabella, Elisa, illustrator.
Title: Please explain divorce to me! : because my parents are breaking up
  -- a story for children and step-by-step guide for parents / by Laurie
  Zelinger, PhD, Elisa Sabella.
Description: 1st edition. | Ann Arbor, MI : Loving Healing Press, [2024] |
  Includes bibliographical references. | Audience: Ages 5-8 | Audience: Grades K-1 | Summary: "Because divorce
or separation in cohabitating   relationships is a family event, this book was written for both children and adults.
We begin with an engaging story and colorful illustrations for children. Gently telling their children that they
will be getting a divorce, a mother and father share their family story: the journey from their happy wedding
day, through the conflict at present and into the near and reassuring future. The book's second half highlights
important DOs and DON'Ts for parents and provides them with a framework for delivering the difficult news, as
well as a glimpse of what goes through the mind of a child when they are told about an impending divorce"--
  Provided by publisher.
Identifiers: LCCN 2023057539 | ISBN 9781615997800 (paperback) | ISBN
  9781615997817 (hardcover) | ISBN 9781615997824 (epub)
Subjects: LCSH: Divorce--Juvenile literature. | Divorced parents--Juvenile
  literature. | Children of divorced parents--Juvenile literature.
Classification: LCC HQ819.5 .Z45 2024 | DDC 306.89--dc23/eng/20240108
LC record available at https://lccn.loc.gov/2023057539

Published by
Loving Healing Press
5145 Pontiac Trail
Ann Arbor, MI 48105

www.LHPress.com
info@LHPress.com

Tollfree 888-761-6268

Distributed by
Distributed by Ingram Book Group (USA, Canada, UK, EU)

Audiobook available on iTunes and Audible.com

LOVING
HEALING
PRESS

For families everywhere who will be experiencing divorce.

Contents

Introduction

This book was written for families who will be going through a divorce. The first section is a children's story depicting a family where parents reveal they will be getting a divorce. The second part of the book, a parent guide, includes a method for explaining the divorce process to children and helps parents understand what their children are experiencing. While divorce creates significant family upheaval in so many areas, this book is written to help parents recognize that children need to remain their highest priority.

Written by a child psychologist, "Please Explain Divorce to Me" uses a story telling technique that Dr. Zelinger has developed to gently describe the evolution of a family's history from the parents' wedding day, through the joyful birth of their children, leading to the current discord witnessed by the children, and then to the ultimate decision to get divorced. Dr. Zelinger stresses that a healthier divorce is one that leads to better outcome for the children. As such, she provides explicit Do's and Don'ts for parents to follow to improve the adjustment of their children and to set the stage for a co-parenting alliance, despite their feelings for each other. When parents approach the divorce process thoughtfully and with understanding, it helps maintain their child's trust in them and provides support to children as their world changes.

Hi, my name is Simone, and these are my little brothers, Jake and Bodhi. We live with our Mom and Dad and our big fluffy dog, Maxwell, but we call him Max for short. This is the story of our family.

It all started a long-time ago when my Mom and Dad went on a date. They fell in love, got married and had three kids.

Our family did so many fun things together. We went to the playground, the beach, amusement parks and sometimes on vacation. And, of course, we did boring things, too. There were even lots of times we just stayed home with nothing to do. Sometimes, I would fight with my brothers and sometimes they bothered me. Little kids can be so annoying! But Mom and Dad made sure that we always made up.

Mom and Dad also got into fights with each other sometimes. They used to say mean words in loud voices. They didn't know that I was listening but I could hear them arguing. One night I got so scared I started to cry. Mom came into my room and said, "Don't worry, we are just having a disagreement; everything will be okay."

But the next day it happened again. Mom and Dad were shouting in their bedroom. Baby Bodhi was crying, Max was barking like crazy and Jake ran to hide. Even though their door was shut and I covered my ears, I could still hear them yelling. I didn't like this one little bit.

Finally, the screaming ended, and Mom and Dad went to different rooms. They barely spoke to each other. It got way too quiet in our house. I didn't like it this way either.

I was glad when Sunday finally came, because Mom took us to a birthday party but Dad decided to go somewhere else. Hmm. That was a little weird. And when he came home later he slept in Jake's room. Why? I was worried and had trouble sleeping that night.

The next morning, Dad woke Jake and me up for school. He made us breakfast, packed our lunches, checked that we brushed our teeth and took us to the bus stop. I didn't get it. Those are Mom's jobs. Wait, what? Why are things changing? What's going on around here?

For a while after that, some things stayed the same, like how rainbow ices were still my favorite, how I always liked doing cartwheels and how it was my job to walk Max after school. But some things were definitely changing. Mom and Dad stopped taking us places together. It was either Mom or Dad. But not both.

And then came the very worst day of my life!! Mom and Dad called us into the living room and we all sat down on the floor, like we used to when we played games. But this time, the look on their faces told me it wasn't going to be fun, like family game night. Nah-uh.

Dad started the conversation and said, "I want to tell you the story of our family. A long time ago, I met this wonderful woman I wanted to be with." Then he whispered to us, "Guess who I'm talking about? Can you tell its mommy?" and we all laughed. "We fell in love, got married and decided we wanted to have children."

"First, we had a little girl, and we named her Simone. Then, we wanted a boy, and we got Jake. Then, Mommy and I said to each other, 'Wouldn't it be great if we could have one more child in our family?' and we got our wish. Baby Bodhi was born. We were one big family and we loved each other."

Next, it was Mom's turn to talk. "We always did regular things that families **have** to do, like work, laundry, car pool and shopping, but we also did things that were fun." She laughed and said, "Remember the water park we went to last year? Daddy and I love being your parents so much. We will love you forever."

It was quiet for a while before Mom spoke again. "Daddy and I have something to tell you that you probably won't like to hear. If you want to come and sit closer and cuddle with us, you can. This is going to be a serious conversation." I did NOT want to hear it. My heart was beating fast.

Mom began by saying, "You probably noticed that Daddy and I aren't getting along very well these days and we don't agree on very much. Sometimes, we get on each other's nerves and scream a lot when we're together, so we prefer to spend time away from each other. That's why usually only one of us has been taking care of you guys at a time."

Dad said, "I know that you heard us yelling. I'm sorry. We didn't want that to happen. Mom and I have been trying to keep our arguments private but when we have **BIG** feelings, we haven't been doing a very good job of arguing quietly. When we are apart, or separated, we are much happier and better as parents."

Even though Mom and dad weren't agreeing on most things they both agreed that it would be best if they stayed apart from each other but not from us. That meant things would have to change. They would share us. Only one of them would live in this house, and one would go somewhere else to live. We would have two homes.

Mom and Dad would get unmarried and we couldn't change that, but we would still be a family. That's called **divorce**. Mom would always be our mom and Dad would always be our dad. No matter where they lived they would always love us the same amount. Forever.

SEPTEMBER

Sunday	Monday	Tuesday	Wednseday	Thursday	Friday	Saturday
	1 Mom	2 Mom Dad	3 Mom	4 Mom	5 Mom	Mom
7 Mom	8 Mom	9 Mom	10 Dad	11 Mom	12 Mom Dad	Dad
14 Mom	15 Mom	16 Mom	17 Dad	18 Mom	19 Mom	Mom
21 Dad	22 Mom	23 Mom	24 Dad	25 Mom	26 Mom Dad	Dad
28 Dad Mom	29 Mom	30 Mom				

Dad explained that they still agreed on important things, like wanting to spend as much time as possible with us, taking care of us and doing the kind of things we usually did. Figuring out how to divide the time between two homes can be tricky. Since Mom and Dad both wanted to be with us, they would have to make a schedule and decide when we would be with each of them.

I know that sometimes parents don't agree on rules or a schedule. If they can't work it out, they can get help from special people called lawyers, mediators or judges, whose job is to help parents figure out how to share their time with their kids. We might be asked what we would like to see but since we're still young, we don't actually get to make that decision. The grown-ups do.

Ever since we found out about the divorce, Jake and I wondered why it was happening. He thought it might be because he kept missing soccer goals or maybe because the teacher called when he got into a fight at school. I wondered if it was because Bodhi cried and woke everyone up at night. Or maybe it was because of something I did. We were trying so hard to be good.

Jake and I tried to figure out why they were getting a divorce so maybe we could stop it. I asked Mom and Dad but they told me it was nothing that any of us did and it was not our fault. Even when parents get angry with their kids, they never stop loving them or get divorced from them. They were just getting divorced from each other.

Dad said he would probably live at Grandma's house for a while until he found just the right place for the four of us. He would still drive me to dance lessons and take Jake to soccer. And, in the meantime, he would make sure that Grandma's freezer had rainbow ices, since that was still my favorite. When this big family talk was over, we cried and hugged and then played for a while— together.

I don't like these changes, but I will still have a family with a mother, father, two brothers and a big, fluffy dog. But now that I will have two homes, some things might be different. It might take a while to get used to, but I know that Mom and Dad will always do their best to take care of us.

Mommy and Daddy don't love each other the same way anymore, and there isn't anything we can do about it, but they will love me, Jake and Bodhi forever. And I ❤ that.

Real Kids' Drawings About Divorce

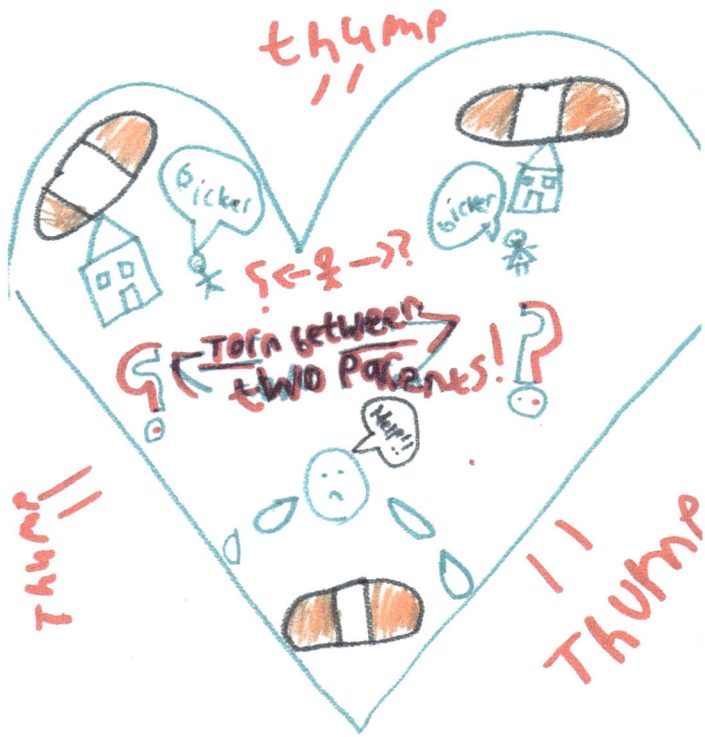

A guide for parents of young children

"Divorce" comes from the Latin word "divortium" meaning separation, and is defined in the Merriam-Webster Dictionary as, "the action or an instance of legally dissolving a marriage". This definition is purely a legal one and does not allude to the emotional toll it takes upon the family or the end of other meaningful unions which may have created families without ceremonial or legal ramifications. Yet, the end of any domestic relationship can be devastating for a family.

Some parents often justify that they are staying in a marriage for the sake of the kids. According to the American Psychological Association, "Divorce can be a traumatic experience for children, but research suggests that most children adjust well within two years following the divorce: on the other hand, children often experience more problems when parents remain in high-conflict marriages instead of splitting up" (Herrick et al., 2013). This parent section will address how to support young children in a family when the parent figures in their life have decided to separate.

Statistics

Almost 50% of all marriages in the United States will end in divorce or separation

* 40% of divorcing couples in the United States have children; over 60% of couples do not
* 20% of marriages end in the first 5 years
* 32% end in the first 10 years
* 48% end in 20 years
* 41% of first marriages end in divorce
* 67% of second marriages end in divorce
* 74% of third marriages end in divorce
* 14% of Lesbian marriages end in divorce
* 7% of Gay Male marriages end in divorce
* 17% increase in divorce rates is seen in families with twins or triplets
* Nearly 50 percent of children in the USA will witness their parents' divorce

Although overall divorce rates had been coming down over the past few decades, the Corona virus pandemic, with its lockdown isolation and concomitant stressors witnessed a 34 % increase rise in divorce statistics in the first few months, especially among those couples who most recently wed. "In fact "20% of couples who had been married for five months or less sought divorce during this time period, compared with only 11% in 2019" (Brownwell, 2020) and even lower rates in the preceding years.

If you are among those families who will be divorcing, you will be faced with many decisions in the months ahead. Helping your children adjust to the upcoming change **must** become your highest priority.

How and What to Tell the Kids

It is understandable that parents approaching divorce may want to spend as much time apart from each other as possible and moments of civility may even be rare. However, if both parents can work together to accomplish the important milestone of informing the children as a team, then doing so would be the preferred option. This sends the message that the parents are in agreement about the divorce, it reduces the child's longing to deny it or talk them out of it and it lets them know that when necessary, parents can put aside their differences to be there for their kids. It also creates the groundwork for learning how to co-parent. Although most children want to see their parents remain together at any cost, only 10-15 % of divorced parents reconcile (Buscho, 2022).

It is recommended to have "the talk" early in the day and without time pressures or distractions so that any questions that may arise can be dealt with throughout the day. Find a comfortable place to talk, where you can be free to hug or hold your child if they need it. Keep it informal. Since children often sit and play on the floor, joining them in their comfort zone can be an option. Many parents tend to have meaningful talks with their children at bedtime, however this should not be one of those times or topics. Powerful, life changing information delivered at bedtime can affect sleep.

The contents of "the talk" should be discussed between both parents in advance. It is detrimental for a child to feel they must show loyalty to one parent over another so keep in mind that the children should not know who wronged whom. Therefore, it is critical that parents avoid placing blame on one another where the children are concerned. Rather, remain as neutral as possible and explain that this decision has already been made. The place to discuss your own anger or sadness is with another trusted adult or therapist- not with your children! Accept your child's reactions, validate their feelings and provide reassurance that you know how hard it is and you will help them through it. Don't try to avoid their discomfort or distract them from their feelings since you would only be postponing the inevitable, perhaps to a time when you are less prepared to deal with it.

The children's story you have just read supplies a framework and sequence for the discussion you will have with your children beginning with

1) how you met

2) your wedding day

3) having children

4) family activities

5) the current situation marked by marital conflict

6) the future, including any information you are relatively sure of as well as what will improve once the divorce has happened.

As a child psychologist, I developed this technique in my private practice and use it with the divorcing families I treat, making sure to gather background information so as to personalize the story for their individual circumstances. Recounting the evolution of the family story to your children serves several functions:

- Children love to hear about their past, especially when they were a baby.
- It reaffirms to children that their parents originally formed their union because they cared for each other.
- The review of the birth of each child reinforces to the child that they were appreciated and their birth was a happy event.
- The evolution of the story from the beginning to the present time as well as discussion of the current friction in the marriage serves to introduce this weighty information more gently than just announcing the news out of the blue, and confirms for children that their perceptions of parental discord are indeed accurate.
- The description of the future helps a child learn what to expect and reassures them that even with change, they will be cared for.

Regardless of how parents decide to tell their kids, children often remember elements of the way they "found out" many years later. While there is no easy way to do this, I found that parents are appreciative and relieved when they have a structure to follow. This method offers a caring vehicle for delivering life changing news.

Children want to Know

- Why are you getting divorced?
- What's going to happen?
- Is it something I did?
- Where will I live? What about Mom and Dad? When will I see them?
- What will the new home be like?
- Will I see my friends?
- How will I get to school?
- Who will buy me what I want and need?
- Will Mom and Dad get back together?
- How am I supposed to act?
- Has this happened to anyone I know?
- What should I tell my friends?
- Can I prevent the divorce from happening?
- If you hate each other, will you still love me?

Addressing their concerns

If you can anticipate any of these questions, you can be prepared to answer them and if you don't know, it is perfectly fine to say so. It is best to keep your answers basic and wait to see what your child brings up.

Allow your child their true reactions without trying to dismiss, distract or minimize their feelings. It can certainly be uncomfortable but it is indeed necessary for the child to know they can express themselves and that their parents can handle and accept those emotions. This helps children maintain their trust in their parents. While it is important for parents to be honest with the information they share, they must only tell the children what they need to know (i.e. what is in their best interests) however tempting it may be to have the child see their side of the story.

It is also acceptable for a child to witness your genuine emotions should you become overwhelmed at any time. While you want to make sure not to blame your spouse for your emotional state, it would be honest to say that you feel sad sometimes but that's okay and you will be fine. Reassure your child that they do not have to take care of you.

Children's reactions to the news

A child's response to hearing about their parent's divorce can be as individual as is each child. Some research indicates that divorce can be more devastating to a child than death. A long term study by Lewis Terman of Stanford University researching the effects of parental divorce and death upon children began in 1921 and was renamed The Longevity Project when it was taken over by Drs. Martin and Friedman in 1956. They compared the effects of divorce to the death of a parent, and discovered that children were more adversely affected by divorce, a seminal research study prompting much interest over decades (Bussemakers et al., 2022; Clark, 2011; Morrow-Kondos, 2016; & Tabeka et al., 2016).

Divorce can be devastating and a child's short term reactions may include anxiety, separation anxiety, sleep or eating problems, depression, guilt, withdrawal, anger, regression, acting out behavior problems, clinginess, health concerns and a decline in academic performance. While some issues might be short lived, others may take longer to resolve. Most children adjust within two years following divorce but if you have lingering concerns consult your child's medical provider or licensed mental health professional.

DO'S:

- Keep arguments private. Divorce can be an ugly, acrimonious process and children must be shielded from open expressions of rage. That means parents have to manage their own feelings if children are their priority. Open hostility is fuel for an unhealthy divorce.
- Keep a calendar in a central location, at the child's eye level, so they know their schedule and where they will be on any given day. It is best to identify change days with different colors or symbols.
- Keep (visitation) drop-offs short.
- Maintain consistency with rules and the order of routines as much as possible within your home and when comfortably possible, across homes (i.e. bathing, teeth brushing, book, bedtime). Consistency brings comfort.
- Keep your child's favorite foods, books and toys on hand so their new home will feel familiar. You may have to buy doubles.
- In a perfect world, it should be the goal of both parents to help the child have two homes where they feel welcome and cared for. Of course, if one parent is incapable then professional consultation is advised regarding how to support the children through this adjustment.
- Notify your child's teacher so they can be attuned to changes in your child and inquire whether the school has a program for children whose parents live separately. Often they are run by school psychologists, social workers, guidance counselors or mental health counselors during lunch or free periods within the school day.
- Consider using an app that provides a shared family platform to facilitate co-parenting communication

DON'Ts

- Don't bash your former spouse (your "ex"). And don't let the grandparents/aunts/uncles do that either. Even subtly.
- Don't let your child be privy to information that is meant for adults. Even if you don't directly tell them anything of a personal nature, children often pick up information by overhearing conversations and phone calls, reading texts and interpreting body language. Be careful.
- Don't send subtle passive-aggressive hints to your child in an attempt to align their feelings with your own. Besides derailing your child's trust and love in a second parent, the child may assume that any similar traits they have to either parent may become an irritant to the opposite parent, creating an underlying worry that the child may likewise become rejected.
- Do not introduce your children to new love interests until you are sure that a new relationship is moving forward. Casual dates should not be foisted upon children who are adjusting to a new normal. Besides, if that new relationship dissolves, your children will be experiencing another loss. You want to protect them from that.

Summary:

Divorce, a common social occurrence that had been slowly declining prior to the Corona virus pandemic in 2020, has since witnessed a reversal with divorce now on the rise. Regardless of whether your union can be described as a legal marriage, a domestic partnership or something else, when two parents part, children are affected. Research shows that open hostility and high conflict are more damaging to children than divorce. Therefore, doing what is best for the children may mean that you have made the decision to separate.

Helping your child adjust to a new family structure and meeting their needs should be your highest priority. While it may be tempting to act cavalierly in a misguided attempt to minimize the event for your child, don't do it. Children need to be handled gently, thoughtfully and with keen understanding of their feelings. You have built their world, and you need to continue to meet their needs with love, support and reassurance. A careful, well planned approach toward preparing them for the news, the move, and beyond will improve your chances of creating a healthier divorce for the entire family.

References

Brownwell, T. (2020, October 16). *Divorce rates and COVID-19.* The National Law Review, 10(290), https://www.natlawreview.com/article/divorce-rates-and-covid-19.

Buscho, A.G. (2022, June 7). *Why many divorced couples end up remarrying each other.* Reviewed by Abigail Fagan for Psychology Today, https://www.psychologytoday.com/intl/blog/better-divorce/202206/why-many-divorced-partners-remarry-each-other.

Clark, R. (2011, May 5). *A Connection Between Parental Divorce and Death?* Longevity Project: Parental divorce biggest social predictor of early death. Retrieved October 16, 2022 from https://www.psychologytoday.com/us/blog/mothering-nature/201105/connection-between-parental-divorce-and-death.

Bussemakers,C., Kraaykamp,G., Tolsma, J. (2022, March 31). *Variation in the educational consequences of parental death and divorce: The role of family and country characteristics.* Demographic Research: Volume 46, Article 20. Retrieved October 16, 2022 from https://www.demographic-research.org 607.

Herrick, L., Haight, R., Palomares, R., & Bufka, L. (2013). *Healthy Divorce- How to Make your split as smooth as possible.* American Psychological Association, *Retrieved Oct 3, 2022, from* https://www.apa.org/topics/divorce-child-custody/healthy.

Morrow-Kondos, D. (2016, July 27). *How kids see Death and Divorce.* TulsaKidsMagazine. Retrieved October 7, 2022 from www.tulsakids.com/how-kids-see-death-and-divorce/.

Merriam-Webster (n.d.). *Merriam-Webster.com dictionary.* Retrieved Oct 16, 2022, from https://www.merriam-webster.com/dictionary/divorce.

Tebeka, S., Hoertel, N., Dubertret, C. & Le Strat, Y. (2016). *Parental Divorce or Death During Childhood and Adolescence and Its Association With Mental Health.* The Journal of nervous and mental disease. 204. 10.1097/NMD.0000000000000549. www.ncbi.nlm.nih.gov/pmc/articles/PMC6313686/

About the Author

Dr. Laurie Zelinger is a Board Certified Psychologist and a Registered Play Therapist with over 45 years' experience. As a child psychologist who has retired from working in public schools, Dr. Zelinger runs a busy private practice and writes books that explain difficult concepts to children. Her books for Loving Healing Press include: "Please Explain Anxiety to Me: Simple Biology and Solutions for Children and Parents"; "Please Explain *'Time Out'* to Me: A Story for Children and Do-It-Yourself Manual for Parents"; "Please Explain Vaccines to Me Because I Hate Shots!"; "Please Explain Alzheimer's Disease to Me: A Children's Story and Parent Handbook About Dementia"; "Please Explain Tonsillectomy & Adenoidectomy to Me: A Complete Guide to Preparing Your Child for Surgery"; "Please Explain Terrorism to Me! A Story for Children and P-E-A-R-L-S of Wisdom for Their Parents"; and Baby Bandage & His First Aid Family: Healing Little Hurts and Booboos". Dr. Zelinger has also worked with American Girl where she produced "A Smart Girl's Guide to Liking Herself Even On The Bad Days" and she is credited with being a consultant for their Bitty Baby book series where she assisted in the development of the *'For Parents'* sections. In addition, Dr. Zelinger has written for Play Therapy magazine as well as for therapeutic books where her chapters offer strategies that can be used with fearful children. Dr. Laurie's passion for writing began when she discovered journaling in third grade, and which was then fortified in fourth grade when she wrote a play that was performed by students in her public school.

Dr. Laurie is a Fellow and previous elected officer in the national American Academy of School Psychology, following four years as Director on the Executive Board of the New York Association of Play Therapy and she has contributed to nearly 200 venues regarding child development. Dr. Laurie and her psychologist husband, Dr. Fred, are both certified Red Cross Disaster Mental Health volunteers. They have been happily married for over 40 years, have raised four children and relish their roles as grandparents.

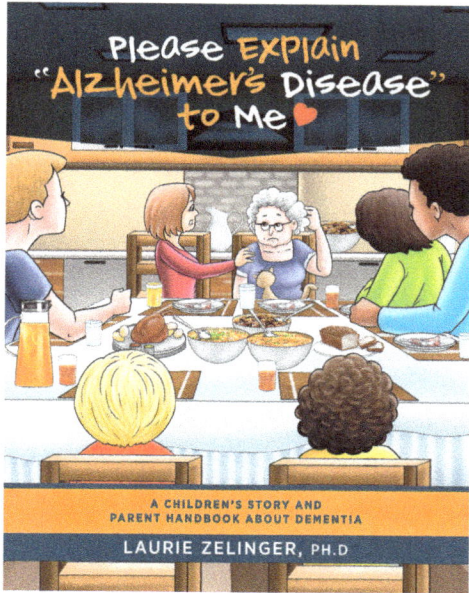

Please Explain "Alzheimer's Disease" to Me ♥

A CHILDREN'S STORY AND PARENT HANDBOOK ABOUT DEMENTIA

LAURIE ZELINGER, PH.D

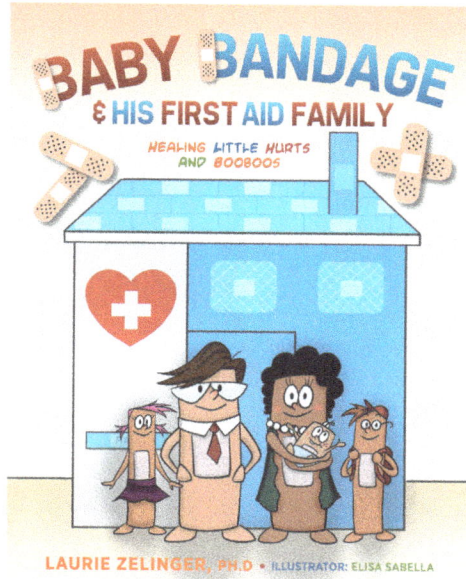

BABY BANDAGE & HIS FIRST AID FAMILY

HEALING LITTLE HURTS AND BOOBOOS

LAURIE ZELINGER, PH.D • ILLUSTRATOR: ELISA SABELLA

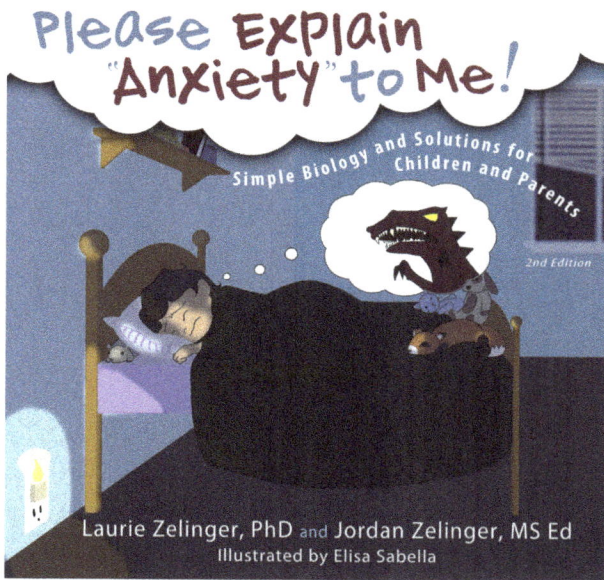

Please EXPLAIN "Anxiety" to Me!

Simple Biology and Solutions for Children and Parents

2nd Edition

Laurie Zelinger, PhD and Jordan Zelinger, MS Ed
Illustrated by Elisa Sabella

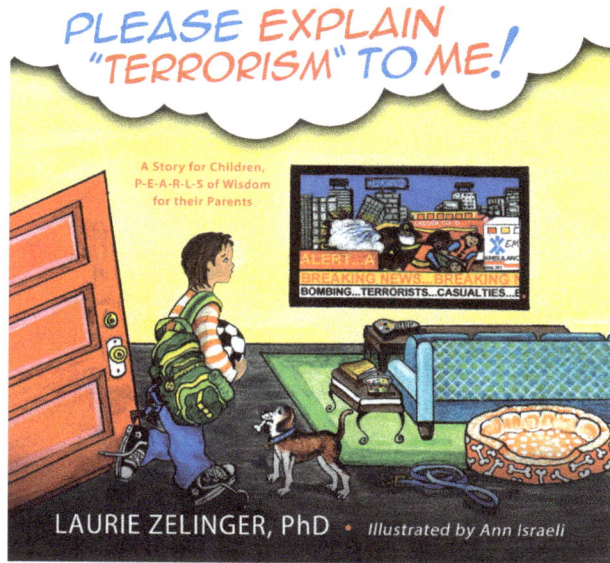

PLEASE EXPLAIN "TERRORISM" TO ME!

A Story for Children, P-E-A-R-L-S of Wisdom for their Parents

ALERT...A BREAKING NEWS...BREAKING
BOMBING...TERRORISTS...CASUALTIES...E

LAURIE ZELINGER, PhD • Illustrated by Ann Israeli

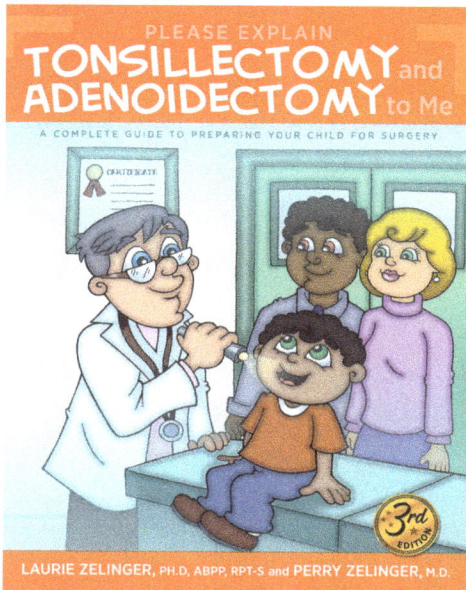

PLEASE EXPLAIN TONSILLECTOMY and ADENOIDECTOMY to Me

A COMPLETE GUIDE TO PREPARING YOUR CHILD FOR SURGERY

3RD EDITION

LAURIE ZELINGER, PH.D, ABPP, RPT-S and PERRY ZELINGER, M.D.

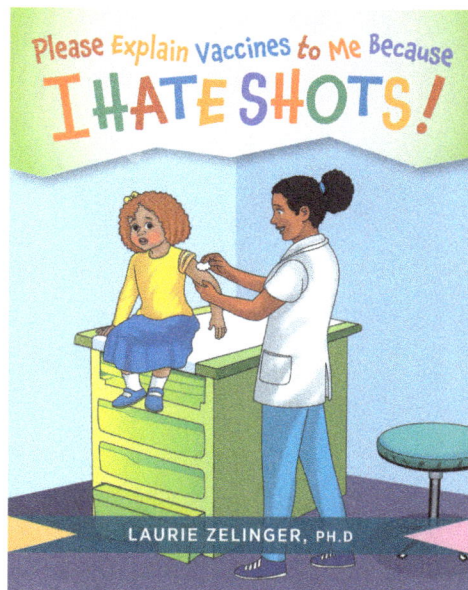

Please Explain Vaccines to Me Because I HATE SHOTS!

LAURIE ZELINGER, PH.D

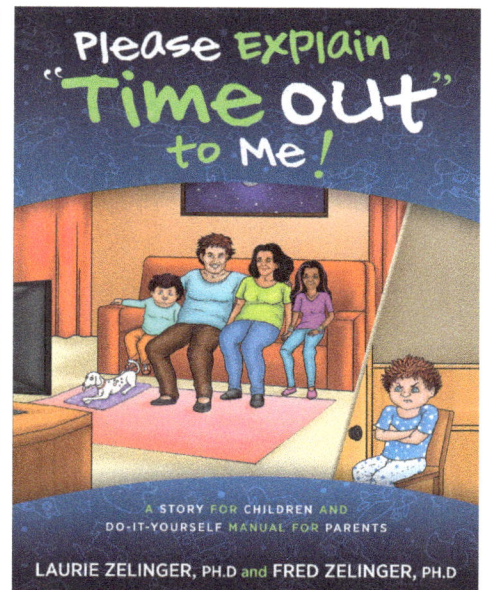

Please EXPLAIN "Time Out" to Me!

A STORY FOR CHILDREN AND DO-IT-YOURSELF MANUAL FOR PARENTS

LAURIE ZELINGER, PH.D and FRED ZELINGER, PH.D